Weeds, Pests and Diseases

Cullen Garden Guides

Weeds, Pests and Diseases

by Mark Cullen

Summerhill Press Ltd.
Toronto

© Mark Cullen

Published by Summerhill Press Ltd
            Toronto, Ontario

Cover Photography: Dieter Hessel
Editors: Tony Reynolds
            Judith Drynan
Illustrations: Gill Cameron

Canadian Cataloguing in Publication Data

Cullen, Mark, 1956-
  Weeds, pests and diseases

(Cullen garden guides)
ISBN 0-920197-11-6.

1. Weeds. 2. Garden pests. 3. Plant diseases.
I. Title. II. Series.

SB611.C84 1985   632   C85-098343-6

Distributed in Canada by:
Collier Macmillan Canada
50 Gervais Drive
Don Mills, Ontario M3C 3K4

Printed and Bound in Canada

The busy bee teaches two lessons: one is not to be idle, and the other is not to get stung.

Contents

Lady Bug/Leaf Cutting Bee/
Leaf Miner/Leaf Roller/
Leafhopper/Mexican Bean
beetle/Mealy Bug/Preying
Mantis/Rose Chafer/Sawfly/
Scale/Slugs and Snails/Sow-
bug/Spider Mites/Squash
Vine Borer/Tent Caterpillar/
Thrips/Tomato Hornworm/
Weevil/Whiteflies/Wire
Worms

Letter From Mark

Mother Nature meant this world to balance perfectly. Without the interference of man, every plant, insect and animal has a place in a never-ending circle of life which wastes nothing. This fact is sometimes difficult for me to keep in mind when a swarm of mosquitoes is trying to drain me one tiny sip at a time, or a deer fly has just given me a sharp bite right between my toes.

When this balance is upset, in monoculture, for example, when one crop is planted exclusively, more insects and diseases spring up to put it right again, and we get infestations like the outbreaks of spruce budworm in softwood forests.

A backyard garden is a far cry from monoculture, but not far enough away to keep pests from trying to harvest your crop before you do — often mere hours after you plant.

In this book, I describe the signs and symptoms of possible trouble, show you what some of the insects and weeds look like, and talk about preventions and remedies. Very often we tend to look for exotic explanations to very simple problems. Some people, when hearing hoofbeats, will look for zebras instead of horses, but in gardening the problems are usually basic and simple. If you suspect something may be more complicated, if you actually see some zebras, you can take part of the afflicted plant to a nursery, a Ministry of Agriculture Office, or a company which produces pesticides. They have experts who will tell you what the situation and solution is.

This is what I did when my father-in-law had some difficulty with a double row of ash trees lining his driveway. One spring, the new leaves started to fall off for no apparent reason. They didn't seem to be afflicted with any disease, and they certainly weren't being chewed by insects. It was almost as if the tree suddenly thought it was September. I went to the people at Green Cross and they were able to diagnose the problem. The weather was simply too hot and dry for the sensitive leaves on those trees, so they were giving up and falling off. In a few weeks the trees were back to normal again, and the problem turned out to be much simpler to discover than to pronounce. In fact, the only lasting shock effect was the one some listeners of my radio programme sustained when I mentioned the name of the affliction . . . bare ash disease.

When you're looking for a cause, start simply. And when you're correcting a problem, be gentle. In your backyard you can cure with a little bit of medicine at the right time, and help keep nature's balance on an even keel.

Happy Gardening,

Mark Cullen

Chapter One

Prevention

Prevention

My primary rule of green thumb with insect and plant disease problems is, an ounce of prevention is worth a ton of cure. A close second would be — give your garden exactly what it needs, no less and no more, for the production of healthy growth.

The Sticky-Fingered Blight is a two-footed pest which makes off with your produce just when it ripens.

Although there are many pests in the garden, one of the most common is the two-footed human variety. They usually fall into three categories: The Sticky-Fingered Blight, The Heavy-Handed Havoc, and The Procrastinating Pest.

The Sticky-Fingered Blight strikes when harvest reaches its peak — when the smell of cantaloupe fills the air and wafts out to eager noses throughout the neighbourhood, when apples are red, juicy, and beckoning, and when you can almost hear the sound of plump ripe raspberries falling to earth on a summer evening. This is when Sticky Fingers can steal in and take your goodies out from under your very nose.

The second strain usually occurs with the ministrations of the gardener who concludes that if one dose of fertilizer is good, a double dose will be twice as good. The damage continues when everything the plants require — light, water, pruning — is overdone. Heavy-handedness not only wreaks havoc — it wrecks plants.

The third strain, The Procrastinating Pest, always waits until it's too late before attacking the weeds or watering the lawn. Plants get less attention than they should and suffer because of it.

Once the two-footed pests are brought under control, the other varieties can be dealt with.

Nowhere is the adage about an ounce of prevention truer than it is in the garden. It all starts with a good knowledge of what individual plants need. Some have very specific requirements while others are more flexible, but all can be put under stress if the water conditions, drainage, light and fertilizer are excessive or limited. As soon as plants are put under stress, pests and diseases start to attack. Always remember that a healthy plant has a very good chance of resisting predators and weakening diseases.

While each plant is individual in its requirements, here are some general suggestions for minimizing problems.

Soil

Most plants thrive in friable (easily crumbled) soil with a good proportion of organic material in it. Soil with too much clay prevents water from draining and

---

THE PERFECT TREE

The Ginko, after many millions of years of resisting blights, diseases, viruses, and insect infestations, has become the almost perfect tree. Native to areas in China, the Ginko is completely hardy up to Zone 4 (as far north as North Bay, Winnipeg, and Quebec City) and is virtually insect and disease free.

---

dries to a rock-hard state that can strangle roots. On the other hand, earth which is too sandy lets water flush away before the roots can absorb what they need for the plant to survive, and the soil shifts around so much when it dries that the plants often become uprooted. Organic material, such as peat moss, composted manure, and leaf mold, opens up clay soil and can also give sandy mixtures something to hang onto. Because particles of organic material are large and irregularly shaped, they let water drain well, and because they are porous, they also absorb water — holding it long enough for the roots to take up just what they need. Soil for your houseplants and seedlings should be

Amend the soil with organic material to make it easy to crumble.

Check how fast a hole drains before planting a tree or bush.

sterile, and free of fungus spores, insects and weed seeds as well. For the most part, artificial mixtures are better for indoor gardening. They're light, fluffy, organic (when peat moss is included), and sterile. Look for Canadian brand names like Pro Mix, Ready Earth, or Mother Earth.

Water

Every plant needs water, but more plants are damaged by too much than by not enough. As the symptoms are exactly the same in both cases, the first rule about water is adequate drainage. With houseplants, the holes in plant pots must be kept open, so don't put gravel or broken pieces of clay pots in the bottom of the potting containers. The plant roots will keep the soil from trickling out and if these roots start to clog up the hole, replant. If the pot is in a container which does not have drainage holes, take the inner pot out when you water the plant, and don't put it back until the excess has drained away.

Drainage in the garden is just as important. Don't plant in areas where puddles remain long after the rain stops. Before planting a sapling or seedling, fill the hole with water and if it drains within a couple of hours, less time for smaller ones, it will provide a healthy internal environment. Otherwise, seek another site.

When and how often you water depends on the individual needs of the plant, but it usually should be before the leaves start to wrinkle or wilt. How you water is important as well. Most plants prefer to have a lot of water every once in a while rather than a trickle a day. Some plants, like African violets, don't like to get their leaves wet, and roses and beans should always be soaked at ground level to reduce their susceptibility to disease. Plants will need more water when it's bright and sunny or windy and dry, and also when they are growing vigorously. They'll need less when the light is low, when it's cloudy, and when they are resting or dormant. Find out what each plant needs, then use common sense and affection to know when it is thirsty.

Light

Light requirements for plants vary even more than the need for water. The only general rule is that nothing grows in complete darkness, but there is sure to be something which will grow in every degree of light — from a faint gleam to full sunlight. Each plant will tell you when it needs more or less light. If it has smaller than normal leaves with gaps between them, longer than usual stems, and isn't as green as it should be, it needs more light. However, when the uppermost parts of the leaves are scorched, it needs less light. A good rule to follow is that whenever you're changing the light a plant receives, especially if

INSECT EATING PLANTS
The Pitcher Plant and the Venus Flytrap enjoy a high protein diet of living insects. The Pitcher Plant is found mainly in tropical Asia. Its leaves are shaped like vases, or pitchers, and contain a sweet juice called nectar. Insects enter the pitchers to drink the juice, and once inside they are caught by hairs and fall down into the digestive acid at the bottom. The Venus Flytrap is found in the Southern United States. When an insect lands on one of its leaves, tiny little teeth on the edges close together and trap the victim. It's completely digested by juices inside the leaf in about ten days.

Some plants won't bloom if given too much nitrogen, but a lawn without nitrogen contained in a good fertilizer, would hardly survive.

you're moving it from less to more, do it in gradual stages. Too much change all at once can be damaging.

Fertilizer

If all plants were the same, you could just give them a regular fertilizing with 20-20-20 plus trace elements and they would all be happy. Happily, gardening is not that simple. It requires thought. For example, too much nitrogen can cause some plants to grow a number of leaves but no fruit or flowers, while a lawn without any nitrogen at all would hardly survive. Follow specific instructions at first, and then combine them with your own experience and instinct.

Too much fertilizer often causes leaves to have brown dried-up margins, while not enough is often characterized by yellow leaves, poor growth, and few, if any, flowers. In the Cullen Garden Guide For Houseplants I describe the symptoms of specific deficiencies in more detail.

pH

Many plants need soil conditions which are either acid or alkaline. While most will do well in a pH range from 6.0 to 7.5, there are some you have to make adjustments for by testing the pH. Add peat moss, oak leaves, or compost to lower the pH or make it more acidic, and ground limestone in order to raise the pH or make it more alkaline.

Competition

Plants are always competing for the elements necessary for good growth. Annuals and vegetables always do better when they are thinned to give each plant enough room to grow well. Grass and other plants need extra water and nutrition when growing near the roots of thirsty trees like poplars. Weeds provide competition too, and should be eliminated as soon as possible. Proper pruning can reduce competition within the plant itself, and help it provide larger flowers or fruit as well as reducing stress.

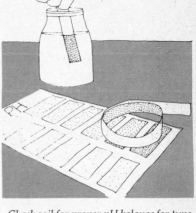

Check soil for proper pH balance for type of plant.

Support

Keeping fruit and vegetables off the ground with trellises, stakes or mulch, saves them from the munches of pests like slugs and snails, and those diseases which thrive in damp earth.

Ventilation

Plants which are susceptible to fungus and mildew will be less likely to fall prey to those diseases if air is allowed to circulate freely around and about them. Ventilation allows foliage to dry off and warm up earlier in the morning and much sooner after a rainfall.

Plants do better when thinned to allow room for growth.

Temperature

This is more likely to be a problem with plants in the house than those out of doors, because many houseplants are tropical in nature and don't react well to sudden changes in temperature like the opening of a door in winter. Sometimes people will be fooled into thinking that the bright sunshine in early spring will be good for their plants and so they place them beside an open window — where the poor things shiver to pieces. Outdoors, plants growing in cooler zones than they do in their natural environment can run into the same problems unless they are given adequate protection.

Resistant Varieties

In an attempt to help nature keep balanced, man has encouraged plants to strengthen resistance to some diseases and pests. You can buy plants which are highly resistant to fusarium wilt, verticillium wilt, rust, and other destructive diseases. Obviously, growing these resistant varieties will give you fewer problems.

Certified Stock

This usually applies to vegetables, especially to varieties of potatoes. If you buy stock which is guaranteed to be free of the various fungus spores, viruses and insect eggs which the seeds or seedlings are most vulnerable to,

Cats and dogs getting into the garden are a never-ending problem, but many of the listeners to my radio programe on CKEY in Toronto have used this recipe to repel these domestic pests:
1 quart of warm water
1 clove garlic or 1 tbsp. of garlic powder
1 onion
1 tbsp. cayenne pepper
$1/_2$ tsp. Tabasco sauce
Mix these ingredients together in a blender, and pour it anywhere outside where dogs and cats might cause a problem. Avoid getting it on tender-leafed annual plants and vegetables.

you'll be much more likely to have a disease-free season. A problem often occurs when people keep seeds from their own vegetables to grow the following season. Some diseases may not have been sufficiently virulent to cause a problem the first year, but they can get a really good grip if the same seeds are planted again.

Rotation

When you plant the same crop in the same place year after year, the pests and diseases know where to find their prey. What happens is that the eggs or spores winter in the soil, and attack the plants the following season. Rotation minimizes this and confuses the enemy. In particular, be sure not to plant any member of the cabbage family—broccoli, brussels sprouts, cauliflower and cabbages—where any of the others grew last year. This is true for the members of the tomato family—tomato, potato, eggplant, and peppers—as well.

Cleaning Up

This is very, very important. Gardens which are kept free of all debris during the growing season are much less likely to have problems. Stuff left lying about, particularly spent flowers, fallen leaves, and ripened fruit not harvested in time, can all harbour pests and diseases which will

DID YOU KNOW?
Electric lightbulbs waste a lot of energy in the form of heat while fireflies and glow worms produce light without wasting any of their energy on heat at all. Their light is produced by certain reactions of chemicals within the insects' bodies, and both flashing and steady lights can be produced from patches on the sides or undersides of the insects to attract one another.

GARDEN FOLKLORE
Early Canadian pioneers believed Lemon Balm, when served as a drink, was soothing to the nerves, comforting to the heart, and cheering to the spirit. Sage was thought to be good for the memory. Camomile, when grown near a sick plant, was believed to have the mysterious power of bringing that plant back to good health.

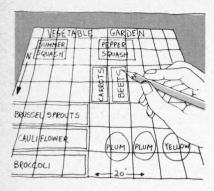

When planning your garden, be sure to rotate members of the cabbage and tomato families every year.

spread. Pick up all extraneous material and discard it immediately. Don't dig it in. Mulch and other soil amendments should come from clean, uninfected and unrelated plants.

Cleanliness also applies at the end of the growing season. As soon as the crop is finished, clean up the leftover stems, leaves and roots. Keep the weeds down, too, even if there is nothing else growing in your garden, so that weed seeds don't plague you the following year.

Get rid of any diseased plant part immediately so it doesn't infect the whole plant.

PLANT DECOYS

Instead of fruit farmers covering all their blackcurrant bushes with a net to protect them from birds, it has long been a custom in parts of England to plant a single white currant bush in every row of blackcurrant bushes, so the birds will eat the sweeter white currants instead.

Surgery

As soon as you notice a leaf, flower or plant that shows signs of a disease, get rid of it so the problems don't infect the rest of your garden. You don't always have to be radical. One rose leaf with black spot doesn't mean the whole plant has to go. Just pick the leaf and spray the rest of the plant with a suitable fungicide.

When you discard an infected plant or part, don't put it on the compost heap. Burn it, if local by-laws permit, or put it in a plastic garbage bag for the trashman.

LEAP LIKE A FLEA

A flea, which is seldom more than a couple of millimeters long and never more than one centimeter long, jumps 50 to 100 times its own length, and three sets of muscles give the flea the ability to jump eight to ten inches up in the air. Proportionately, a full grown man would have to jump 330 feet or 100 metres to leap like a flea.

THE MATING GAME

A female preying mantis will kill and eat her mate if she catches him moving prior to mating. The male creeps up from behind the female, freezing in his tracks every time she turns around, for she will only attack if she sees him move. He'll wait until her attention is distracted and then quickly move in to mate, at which time, the female eats him anyway and devours him in the act of procreation.

Awareness

When you know which pests and diseases are most likely to affect which plants, you can recognize the first signs and stop an outbreak before it becomes a problem. Often you can do it without resorting to chemicals. Taking all these preventive steps will have other advantages as well. You'll be out in the garden enjoying your plants and ready to pick flowers, fruit and vegetables at their peak. You'll notice pests and diseases in the early stages and be able to take the first-step cures, and you'll be able to save yourself the kind of disappointment which comes when plants wither and die needlessly.

SMOKERS TAKE CARE!
A disease deadly to some plants, called 'Mosaic Virus', can be transmitted to susceptible plants like tomatoes, peppers, and eggplant from the fingers of smokers. If you smoke, always be sure to wash your hands *before* you go out to work in the garden.

Chapter Two

Symptoms and Causes

Symptoms and Causes

If all your preventive measures fail and the problem is not as obvious as a large hornworm caterpillar gnawing on your prize beefsteak tomato, look up the symptoms in this chapter. I have listed them by plant part: fruit, flower, leaves, stem and root. Beside each symptom is a list of possible causes which you can then look up in the chapters on pests and diseases. In those chapters you will find the preventive steps you can take and the cures. It is very important that you identify the cause of the problem correctly before you begin to treat it. Otherwise you will be wasting your time and money, and possibly putting the plant under unnecessary stress.

FRUIT

Symptom	Possible Cause
Holes in skin, sometimes surrounded by brown castings.	1. Slugs, snails. 2. Corn borers, corn ear worms, fly larvae. 3. Tarnished plant bugs on apples.
Cracks, open or covered with scar tissue.	1. Fruit may contain insects or slugs but cause is usually stress from uneven water supply like a flooding of water after a dry spell.

Fruit (Continued)

Symptom	Possible Cause
Leathery patches.	1. On the bottom of tomatoes, blossom end rot. 2. On tree fruit, scab, or, if patches are raised, insects such as surface-feeding caterpillars or tarnished plant bugs. 3. On top of soft fruit and tomatoes, sunscald (patches can also be shrunken and soft in this instance). 4. On beans, anthracnose.
Soft brown areas, white powdery deposit.	1. Rot or blight. 2. Mildew, botrytis, advanced stages of rot.
Mishapen.	1. Mildew, botrytis, rot, poor cultural practice.
Small "nubby" strawberries with hard seedy tips.	1. Tarnished plant bugs.

FLOWER

Symptom	Possible Cause
Drop.	1. Sudden change in growing conditions, particularly temperature and water supply. 2. Poor pollination due to cold or lack of pollinating insects. 3. Insufficient light.
Mishapen.	1. Slugs, snails. 2. Caterpillars. 3. Insect adults, such as rose chafers, Japanese beetles, aphids.
Small.	1. Stress caused by poor cultural practice; too little or too much light, water, fertilizer; insufficient pruning.

Flower (Continued

Symptom	Possible Cause
Non-existent.	1. Poor cultural practice or improper preparation of spring flowering bulbs or late pruning of spring flowering shrubs. 2. Insects or diseases on roots (see roots).
Powdery white or grey deposit followed by rotting.	1. Botrytis.

LEAF

Symptom	Possible Cause
Pale or yellow.	1. May be natural, particularly on older leaves or lower leaves of tropical plants. 2. Low light, cool temperatures. 3. Nutrient deficiency, particularly when accompanied by contrasting veins. 4. Early sign of too much light.
Black areas sometimes surrounded by yellow.	1. Black spot.
Large brown patches at leaf margins.	1. Too much fertilizer. 2. Uneven water supply.
Large brown patches on exposed surfaces.	1. Too much sun. 2. Sucking insects under leaf, such as whiteflies, aphids, scale.
Small brown spots.	1. Flea beetles (leaves will also have small holes). 2. Leaf miners (leaves will also have trails). 3. Diseases such as anthracnose, fungus, mold, rust.

Symptom	Possible Cause
Yellow patches.	1. Insects such as white flies, leaf miners, aphids, mites under leaf. 2. Early stages of sunscald. 3. Diseases such as clubroot, virus, mildew.
Silver spots or mottling.	1. Thrips. 2. Leafhoppers.
Purple blotches.	1. Blight (particularly on potatoes and tomatoes).
Wilted.	1. Too little (or too much) water or fertilizer. 2. Poor root action from disease. 3. Frost. 4. Sucking insects under leaf such as whiteflies, aphids, scale. 5. Stem borer (when the whole vine or shoot wilts). 6. Verticillium wilt. 7. Fusarium wilt.
Holes or pieces cut from leaf margins.	1. Insects such as Japanese beetles, earwigs, caterpillars, tarnished plant bugs, weevils, leaf-cutting bees, slugs, snails.
Bronzed or silvery specks.	1. Leafhoppers (severe infestations cause dead areas in leaf).
Curled.	1. Sucking insects such as white flies, aphids, scale. 2. Leaf rollers (if there is a web on leaf). 3. Early stages of wilt (see wilted).
Irregular trails in leaf.	1. Leaf miners.
Powdery deposits.	1. Fungus diseases, mildew, botrytis.
Too small.	1. Insufficient light, fertilizer, virus disease.

STEMS

Symptom	Possible Cause
Long and spindly.	1. Insufficient light, fertilizer.
Bent near end which eventually dies.	1. Stem borer. 2. Canker.
Deposit like soap suds where leaf joins stem.	1. Spittlebugs.
Scaly deposit, cut at ground level.	1. Aphids, scale insects. 2. Cutworms. 3. Damping-off disease, mildew, fungus.
Chewed bark.	1. Mice, rabbits, deer.
Bark cracked or split.	1. Whipped by wind. 2. Dehydration over winter. 3. Sunscald in winter. 4. Too much or too little water or fertilizer. 5. Disease on roots (see roots). 6. Diseases such as scab, canker, botrytis, anthracnose.
Gummy deposit.	1. Borer insect, causing hole in wood under gum.

ROOTS

Symptom	Possible Cause
Black, grey, brown spots, often with soft areas.	1. Diseases, such as botrytis, rot, blight.
Holes.	1. Root maggots, slugs. 2. Borers (particularly in peaches, flowering almonds, purple sandcherry, lilacs).
Cracking and splitting.	1. Poor cultural practice, usually uneven water supply.
Distorted.	1. Poor soil filled with rocks or debris. 2. Clubroot disease. 3. Crown gall disease.

Chapter Three

Weeds

Weeds

Although some weeds are beautiful in the wild, weeds in the garden should never even be permitted to get big enough to identify. They should be removed with a hoe as soon as they poke their heads above ground. In fact, regular cultivation and good mulching can stop them even sooner than that.

Vegetables, especially beets and turnips, need to grow vigorously from germination to harvest for the best taste and texture, and competition from weeds can slow down that vigour. Some of the earliest and best advice Dad gave me during my tenure on our nursery farm was that if you let a weed put down roots and take a firm grip of the soil, most of the pleasure of garden work is gone. Weeds in the lawn are difficult to see early in the season, but a healthy lawn should keep many weeds from germinating.

Prevention is half the battle, but if weeds do manage to get established, here are some ways to identify and deal with them.

Bladder Campion	1. Spreads by seeds and rhizomes. 2. Has a very long root, and will grow back from root sections left in the ground. 3. *Control by hand*: dig out the root, or hoe it over and over again. 4. *Chemical control*: Killex. *NOTE*: 2,4-D, mecoprop and dicamba combine to make up the product Killex, which kills a wide range of broadleafed weeds. Be sure not to spray desirable plants while spraying weeds. Killex will not hurt your lawn when used as directed.

Bladder Campion

Butter and Eggs	1. Spreads by rhizomes. 2. A wild snapdragon with a very pretty flower. 3. *Control by hand*: dig out all the rhizomes. 4. *Chemical control*: Killex.

Butter and Eggs

Canada Thistle	1. Spreads by seeds and rhizomes. 2. Gives wheat farmers problems, because it often takes more than one application of herbicide to get rid of the rhizomes. 3. *Control by hand*: dig out all the rhizomes you can, and watch for new shoots in the same area. 4. *Chemical control*: Killex.

Canada Thistle

Carpet Weed	1. Spreads by seeds. 2. Comes by its name honestly as it can cover a whole garden with one plant. 3. *Control by hand*: pull it out, but make sure you pick up all the widespread stems. 4. *Chemical control*: Killex.

Carpet Weed

36

Chickweed	1. Spreads by seeds. 2. There are two kinds, common and mouse-ear. 3. *Control by hand*: can be pulled out or cut off at roots. 4. *Chemical control*: mecoprop, Killex.

Chickweed

Chicory	1. Spreads by seeds. 2. A pretty blue flower you might want to let grow against a split rail fence. 3. *Control by hand*: pull up but this is hard work as roots have a firm grip. 4. *Chemical control*: Killex, Weed-No-More.

Chicory

Clover	1. Spreads by seeds and natural soil layering of runners. 2. Occasionally used as a ground cover. 3. *Control by hand*: difficult as established plants can have a firm grip. 4. *Chemical control*: mecoprop, Killex, Weed-No-More.

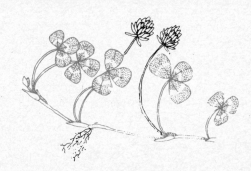

Clover

Common Purslane	1. Spreads by seeds. 2. Thick stems make it visible and easy to identify in lawns. 3. *Control by hand*: can be pulled up quite easily, but must be removed completely as it has an almost unbelievable ability to self-propagate. 4. *Chemical control*: Killex persistently applied, or Hoe-No-More.

Common Parslane

Common Yarrow	1. Spreads by seeds and rhizomes. 2. Fern-like leaves make it easy to identify before it flowers. 3. *Control by hand*: dig up all the rhizomes. 4. *Chemical control*: repeated application of Killex.

Common Yarrow

Crabgrass	1. An annual which spreads by seed. 2. Flourishes in lawns which are under stress from lack of fertilizer and improper seeding and watering. 3. *Control by hand*: if you have the patience, pick out the seeds. 4. *Chemical control*: pre-emergent DCPA, Dacthal. Apply before the lilacs bloom in the spring and the seeds have a chance to germinate.

Crabgrass

Creeping Charlie	1. Spreads by seeds and natural soil layering of runners. 2. Creeps very quickly, and has tiny violet flowers at leaf axils. 3. *Control by hand*: you can dig it out with patience. 4. *Chemical control*: Killex.

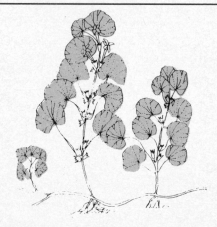

Creeping Charlie

Devil's Paintbrush	1. Spreads by seeds. 2. In a meadow, the orange hawk-weed flowers and red paint-brushes can be quite attractive especially when combined with daisies. 3. *Control by hand*: difficult as roots have the strong grip of most perennials. 4. *Chemical control*: Killex.

Devils Paintbrush

Dandelion	1. Spreads by seeds, sometimes by root division.
	2. Some people use the young leaves in salads and the flowers to make wine.
	3. *Control by hand*: dig all the root out as new plants can grow from the pieces of root you leave behind.
	4. *Chemical control*: Weed-No-More or Killex.

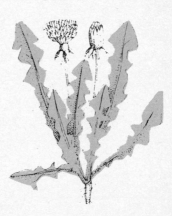

Dandelion

Field Bindweed	1. Spreads by seeds and rhizomes.
	2. Vines can cover a wide area, and tie knots around many plants in the process.
	3. *Control by hand*: separate from other plants, then dig up.
	4. *Chemical control*: Killex.

Field Bindweed

Goldenrod	1. Spreads by seeds.
	2. One of the noxious weeds mentioned in many by-laws as its pollen sometimes causes an allergic reaction in people.
	3. *Control by hand*: it is easy to pull up so do it immediately before the seeds mature.
	4. *Chemical control*: Killex (repeated applications necessary for mature plants).

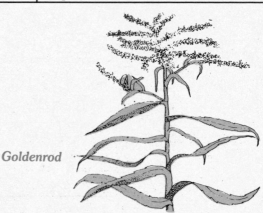

Goldenrod

Horsetail	1. Spreads by spores and rhizomes.
	2. A very old plant, it has its print in fossils.
	3. *Control by hand*: difficult, important to dig up all the rhizomes.
	4. *Chemical control*: Killex (will take more than one application).

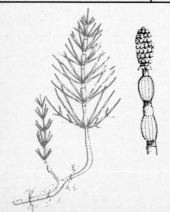

Horsetail

42

Lamb's Quarters	1. Spreads by seeds. 2. *Control by hand*: fairly easy to pull up as roots are not deep. 3. *Chemical control*: Killex.

Lamb's Quarters

Mallow	1. Spreads by seeds, root division. 2. Has an attractive flower, similar to the Rose of Sharon. 3. *Control by hand*: difficult, perennial varieties have a strong grip. 4. *Chemical control*: 2,4-D, mecoprop or Killex.

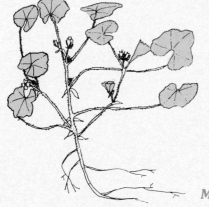

Mallow

Plantain	1. Spreads by seeds.
	2. Crushed leaves can relieve wasp and bee stings.
	3. *Control by hand*: usually easy, but can be difficult in compacted soil.
	4. *Chemical control*: 2,4-D or Killex.

Plaintain

Poison Ivy	1. Spreads by seeds and rhizomes.
	2. Causes an allergic reaction in most people — occasionally quite severe — with even the smoke from the plants, if burned, causing a reaction.
	3. *Control by hand*: not advisable because of the toxicity.
	4. *Chemical control*: 2,4-D or Killex.

Poison Ivy

44

Quackgrass	1. Spreads by rhizomes, sometimes by seed.
	2. This is a real troublemaker for your lawn, especially in its favourite location, beside fences.
	3. Coarse and unattractive, it also grows faster than most other grasses, so it's visible the day after you mow.
	4. Re-seed trouble area annually so healthy grass will push the quackgrass out.
	5. *Control by hand*: important to dig up all the rhizomes.
	6. *Chemical control*: dalapon.

Quackgrass

Queen Anne's Lace	1. Spreads by seeds. 2. It's a wild carrot. 3. *Control by hand*: difficult in compacted soil, but be sure to at least cut off the top of the tap root. 4. *Chemical control*: 2,4-D mecoprop or Killex.

Queen Anne's Lace

Ragweed	1. Spreads by seeds. 2. One of the noxious weeds that by-laws demand people get rid of. 3. *Control by hand*: hard to pull up but hoeing is effective early in season. 4. *Chemical control*: Killex or Weed-No-More (spray while ragweed is young).

Ragweed

46

Redroot Pigweed	1. Spreads by seeds. 2. Very prolific, should be stamped out immediately. 3. *Control by hand*: can be pulled up easily or cut off with a hoe or cultivator. 4. *Chemical control*: 2,4-D or Killex.

Redroot Pigweed

Sow Thistle	1. Spreads by seeds. 2. This has a yellow flower while a Canada thistle is pink. 3. *Control by hand*: the tap root can be difficult to pull up but hoeing is effective on young plants if you get the top of the root. 4. *Chemical control*: 2,4-D or Killex.

Sow Thistle

Chapter Four

Pests

Pests

You have probably heard the old joke about the only thing worse than finding a worm in an apple is finding half a worm, but it seems to be funnier in the telling than in the eating. It's not very amusing to find a cabbage worm on the broccoli you're just about to savour, or an earwig in the salad. It's just as frustrating to inhale a rose chafer when you're taking a deep sniff of a Chrysler Imperial Rose or shake a cloud of whiteflies out of the leaves of your prize fuchsia tree. To prevent these disasters, you have to protect your garden with regular inspection and early treatments.

You have to be pretty fast to beat the bugs though. Cutworms can destroy your whole row of cauliflower seedlings within a few hours of transplanting and slugs can strip all the new blooms off your mums overnight, so you should really check your garden every single day and try to control pests by hand.

Pick caterpillars and other large insects off leaves and drop into a can of water with a film of oil or kerosene on top. Remove those leaves which have been devastated by miners or other insects, as well as the ones covered with aphids or eggs, and get rid of them immediately.

If, for some reason, the pests get ahead of you, you will probably have to call in the heavy artillery in the form of chemical control.

Here is a list of the most common insect and disease problems with recommended treatment — organic first, chemical second.

Organic treatment can range from washing the bugs away with soap and water, to applying controlling products available at any good gardening centre which are produced from natural sources. For example, the ingredient rotenone, used in Deritox Garden Guard comes from the root of a South American plant called cubé.

Great strides have been made in the area of chemical control, and very often the best way to buy the most effective product is by a brand name which contains the ingredients specifically formulated for the problem. A list of these ingredients can be found at the back of the book, but the most important thing to remember when dealing with any chemical solution is to follow the instructions implicitly and keep the spray or dust from settling on healthy plants, people or animals. For this reason you should always use weed or insect killers on a calm day, free of wind. When you use chemicals properly the result can be a finer crop, but trust the experts and do as they suggest for the greatest success.

Aphids	
	1. Like a chameleon, aphids often take on the colour of the plant they infest.
	2. Are most frequently found completely covering new growth but sometimes on mature buds, leaves and fruit.
	3. Will attack almost all plants — flowers, trees, vegetables, fruit.
	4. Garlic and mint planted close by may help keep aphids away from vegetables.
	5. Getting rid of aphids often reduces the number of ants also, as they feed on the sticky secretions of the aphids.
	6. Can be removed from the plant with a strong jet of water, or a spray of insecticidal soap solution.
	7. *Organic control*: Deritox Garden Guard, pyrethrum, Raid House and Garden Spray.
	8. *Chemical control*: malathion, diazinon, Sevin, Guard 'n Pride.

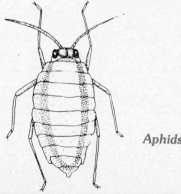

Aphids

Asparagus Beetle	1. Two types, orange with black spots, and striped, feed on asparagus foliage. 2. Both the black-and-white adult and its grey grub larvae can cause problems — the adult (beetle) above ground and the larvae (grubs) below the ground. 3. Usually found on asparagus. 4. Can be picked off by hand, and infestations reduced by removing and burning asparagus tops when they turn brown in the fall. 5. *Organic control*: pulverized lime, Deritox Garden Guard. 6. *Chemical control*: diazinon, Sevin, Guard 'n Pride.

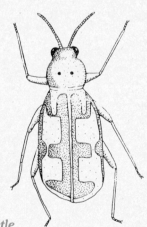

Asparagus Beetle

Cabbage Maggot	1. The larva of a fly which lays its eggs at the base of the stem of cabbage family plants. 2. Likes all members of the cabbage family, broccoli, cabbage, cauliflower, brussels sprouts. 3. Mint, rosemary, and sage planted nearby will help keep maggots at a distance. 4. *Organic control*: wood ashes, spread at the base of the plants can stop the fly from laying its eggs, but a maggot mat is even more effective — a circle of tarpaper set around the base of a newly planted cabbage family seedlings. 5. *Chemical control*: diazinon granuals or liquid, Dylox.

Cabbage Maggot

Cabbage Worm	1. The larva of the small white moth you see fluttering over your cabbage, broccoli, cauliflower and kale.
	2. The larvae prefer the cabbage family, but may also gnaw on many other vegetables including celery, lettuce, peas, and spinach.
	3. Thyme can act as a natural repellant.
	4. *Organic control*: pick them off if infestation is mild, or use regular applications of BT (bacillus thuringiensis) or Deritox Garden Guard applied every seven days.
	5. *Chemical control*: diazinon, Sevin.

Cabbage Worm

Canker Worm	1. One of the green caterpillars nick-named inch worms you see hanging from trees on silk threads. 2. Eats the leaves of trees, especially apple. 3. *Organic Control* : BT (bacillus thuringiensis), Deritox Garden Guard—regular cultivation around the trunk of the tree throughout the summer to dig up the pupae for the birds to eat; a band of something like Tanglefoot around the trunk to keep the adult female from climbing into the branches to lay eggs (only the male insect has wings). 4. *Chemical Control*: diazinon.

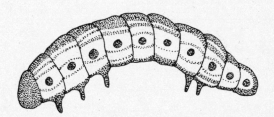

Carrot Worm	1. The larva of the carrot rust fly. 2. Enjoys carrots and parsnips. 3. *Organic control*: rotate crops or skip one season, or plant a late-maturing crop to avoid midsummer egg-laying. 4. *Chemical control*: diazinon.

Carrot Worm

Corn Ear Worm	1. Develops into one of the many moths you'll see fluttering around the porch light. 2. Larvae enter the corn ears from the top, where the silk is, so you don't see the hole in the husk as you would with the corn borer. 3. *Organic Control*: BT (bacillus thuringiensis), pyrethrum; clean up the stalks well at the end of the growing season because this insect will spend the winter there. 4. *Chemical Control*: dust silks with Sevin every three days until harvest.

Corn Ear Worm

Colorado Potato Beetle	1. Both the orange larvae and the black-and-orange adult dine on the foliage of several vegetables — bright orange egg clusters can sometimes be found under leaves. 2. Enjoys all members of the potato family: potatoes, tomatoes, eggplants, peppers. 3. Can be controlled by hand, best if you can find the eggs and get rid of them. 4. *Organic control*: Deritox Garden Guard applied every seven days and after each rainfall. 5. *Chemical control*: Sevin.

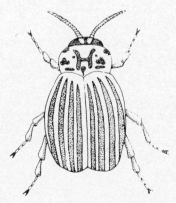

Colorado Potato Beetle

Cucumber Beetle	1. This pest is double trouble, dining on cucumber and leaving a bacterial wilt disease behind it.
	2. Can be found on all the gourds like summer and winter squash and pumpkins.
	3. Radishes planted on hills will repel them, or they can be picked off by hand.
	4. *Organic control*: Deritox Garden Guard.
	5. *Chemical control*: diazinon, Sevin, Guard 'n Pride.

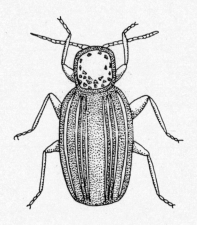

Cutworm	1. It sometimes seems that these insect larvae watch gardeners set out seedlings, then pounce as soon as their backs are turned. 2. Enjoy gnawing the stalks of many newly planted seedlings, particularly tomatoes, cabbages and lettuce. 3. *Organic control*: an effective control is the cutworm collar; a bottomless paper cup placed around the stem of new seedlings and inserted about an inch in the ground. 4. *Chemical control*: Sevin or Banisect.

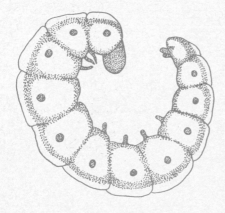

Cutworm

Codling Moth	1. The worm so often found in an apple, having left a large hole in the skin, surrounded by reddish-brown castings. 2. Likes apples and pears. 3. *Organic control*: can be controlled in the off-season with organic dormant oil/sulfur spray. 4. *Chemical control*: spray with Sevin, diazinon, Guard 'n Pride at intervals indicated on the package, starting when the blossom petals have fallen, but never spray insecticides while a tree or shrub is in bloom or you may kill the bees in the trees.

Codling Moth

Dipterous Flies	1. A group of insects which includes the onion maggot, the cabbage maggot and the apple maggot — the worst pest of apples in Eastern Canada. 2. Apple maggot also loves haw-thorns and blueberries. 3. *Organic control*: keep things tidy by cleaning up any apples which fall prematurely and getting rid of them immediately. 4. *Chemical control*: diazinon, Sevin, Cygon 2E.

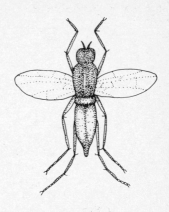

Dipterous Flies

Earwig	1. Does not do a great deal of damage to most plants, but is ugly and the pincers hurt (although they are not strong enough to puncture your skin).
	2. Leave irregularly shaped holes as they eat the leaves of tender flowers.
	3. *Organic control*: diatomaceous earth.
	4. *Chemical control*: Sevin, diazinon, malathion, Banisect.

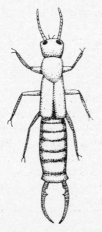

Earwig

Flea Beetle	1. Tiny beetles that jump when disturbed, they eat tiny holes in plant leaves. 2. Enjoy dining on cabbage family, potato family, radishes and turnips, particularly young plants. 3. *Organic control*: pyrethrum, Deritox Garden Guard. 4. *Chemical control*: Sevin, methoxychlor.

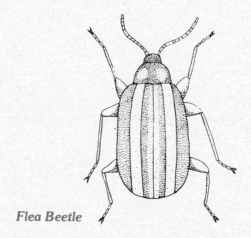

Flea Beetle

Grasshopper	1. This insect has levelled whole wheat fields. 2. Enjoys grassy plants like corn, but will eat almost anything green if there is a lot of competition for food. 3. Seldom becomes a major problem in the backyard. 4. Nasturtiums and chrysanthemums provide a repellent. 5. *Organic control*: pyrethrum, Deritox Garden Guard. 6. *Chemical control*: Sevin, diazinon.

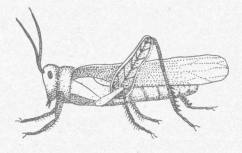

Grasshopper

Japanese Beetle	1. One of the main reasons for strict control of importation of soil, fruits, and vegetables as the adults are very vociferous and meticulous eaters, dining neatly on the flesh between the veins of grape leaves, roses, asparagus, corn, and rhubarb. 2. Grubs attack grass roots. 3. *Organic control*: pyrethrum, Deritox Garden Guard. 4. *Chemical control*: Sevin, on lawns use diazinon, Banisect.

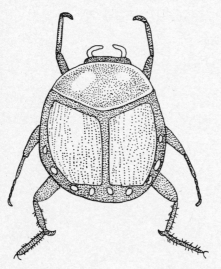

Japanese Beetle

Ladybug	1. Also called the Lady Beetle, this is a beneficial insect, as it dines on aphids.
	2. Sometimes refrigerated boxes of thousands of these insects are available so you can let them loose to clean up the aphids without any kind of spray.

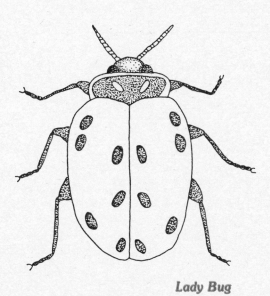

Lady Bug

Leaf-Cutting Bee	1. Cuts well-shaped circles and ovals out of the edges of ornamental plants, particularly roses. 2. Insect does not eat the leaves, but cuts them out to use as nesting material. 3. *Chemical Control* : cabaryl or diazinon may repel them but the damage is usually just a bit unsightly so control is seldom necessary.

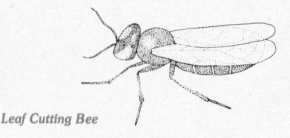

Leaf Cutting Bee

Leafhopper	1. When infestations are well-established, you can see the results of this insect's work on the top of leaves in the form of dead brown patches called hopper burn. 2. Can be found under the leaves of nearly every plant, and can carry potato virus diseases. 3. Nasturtiums and marigolds are repellents. 4. *Organic control*: pyrethrum, diatomaceous earth. 5. *Chemical control*: Sevin, diazinon.

Leaf Miner	1. There is a whole family of miners, nearly one for each plant in the garden, but the damage is always the same; tiny meandering trails eaten out of the leaves of lilacs, chrysanthemums, beets, spinach, and chard.
	2. Birch leaf miners attack birch trees exclusively with the same results.
	3. *Organic control*: remove infected leaves early to keep the miners under control, and weed regularly.
	4. *Chemical control*: malathion, diazinon at regular intervals every two weeks from late May until the end of July. Birch leaf miners — spray Cygon 2E twice each year; the first time in early June, the second in early July — you can also drench soil according to directions or paint full strength on bark of mature birch.

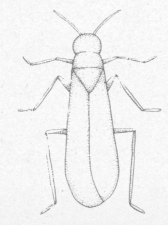

Leafhopper

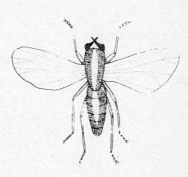

Leaf Miner

Leaf Roller	1. Damage first starts with small holes gnawed in the leaves of fruit trees, chrysanthemums and other plants.
	2. Larvae reside in the leaf, drawing it up with a web frequently found on dwarf and semi-dwarf trees.
	3. *Organic control*: pick the larvae off by hand, Deritox Garden Guard.
	4. *Chemical control*: Sevin, Guard 'n Pride.

Leaf Roller

Mexican Bean Beetle	1. The black sheep of the ladybug family, copper-coloured with 16 black spots.
	2. Causes most damage in the larval stage turning leaves into webs.
	3. Found on all bean plants.
	4. Marigolds and rosemary are repellents.
	5. *Organic control*: Deritox Garden Guard, pick off by hand.
	6. *Chemical control*: Sevin, malathion, or diazinon.

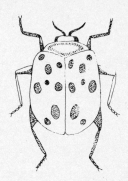

Mexican Bean Beetle

Mealy Bug	1. Usually found in a colony clustered around the leaf axils or under the leaves of many houseplants, including cacti and succulents, wrapped in a waxy silk. 2. *Organic control*: early infections can be picked off by hand, or you can paint infestation with full strength rubbing alcohol. 3. *Chemical control*: the silky covering protects them from topical sprays, systemic insecticides are needed, such as Cygon 2E.

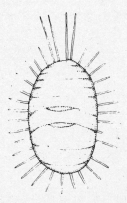

Mealy Bug

Preying Mantis	1. Beneficial insect, quite large and fearsome looking, which enjoys the taste of aphids and many other insects as well. 2. When mature, the preying mantis will kill and eat chinch bugs, crickets, wasps, beetles, flies, tent caterpillars and many others. 3. Occasionally its egg clusters are for sale so you can control your destructive pests naturally.

Preying Mantis

Rose Chafer	1. A light-brown, rounded beetle that particularly enjoys the petals of roses and peonies, although it is not fussy. 2. Grubs can be a problem as they feed on grass roots. 3. *Organic control*: plant onions nearby as repellents, introduce a toad to your rose garden to eat the chafers, and lastly, keep grass out of your garden. 4. *Chemical control*: Sevin, diazinon, malathion.

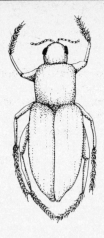

Rose Chafer

Sawfly	1. A family of pests that eat ever-greens, Mountain Ash, fruit trees, and the leaves of roses and goose-berries. 2. Vary in size from tiny leaf miners in birch trees to large caterpillars such as the European pine sawfly. 3. *Organic control*: Spray with Deritox Garden Guard as soon as symptoms appear. 4. *Chemical control*: diazinon, methoxychlor, Cygon 2E.

Sawfly

Scale	1. A family of very small insects which live under protective scales.
	2. Usually found on the bark of trees, they also take up residence under leaves of foliage plants, feeding on sap.
	3. *Organic control*: on trees, spray with dormant oil, lime sulphur in early spring (early April through early May).
	4. *Chemical control*: on leaves, spray with malathion or Cygon 2E late in spring and early in summer.

Scale

Slugs and Snails	1. After the dew has evaporated, you can often see the trails of slime these uglies leave behind.
	2. They eat anything, from lettuce leaves to chrysanthemum flowers.
	3. *Organic control*: can be picked off by hand at night, and cleaning up garden debris helps as it robs them of their daytime resting places — set a saucer of beer on the ground so they will crawl in and drown, or lay down diatomaceous earth.
	4. *Chemical control*: metaldehyde slug bait (keep pets and other living things well away from this) and methiocarb (Trump) which you should keep off plants.

Slugs and Snails

Sowbug (Pillbug)	1. More a nuisance than a pest, these armour-plated bugs roll up in a ball when disturbed, and invade damp basements, cellar window wells. 2. They feed on surface roots and the shoots of newly sprouting plants. 3. *Organic control*: cut a potato in two, hollow out both halves slightly, lay cut surface down on soil — the sawbugs will be attracted to this bait and can then be destroyed: pour boiling water in cracks and crevices: clean up garden debris. 4. *Chemical control*: Sevin, diazinon, Banisect.

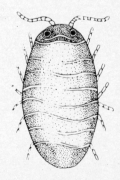

Sowbug

Spider Mites	1. Very small and hard to see, the damage they can do is extensive because of their rapid reproduction.
	2. Can cause mottling and eventually the death of the affected area. Occasionally they will spin very fine webs.
	3. Spider mites enjoy many plants, but are particularly fond of fuchsias, peaches, roses, strawberries, and hibiscus.
	4. Because they reproduce quickly, they can become resistant to chemical controls, so you should alternate two or three different controls.
	5. *Organic control*: lacewings and ladybugs will eat them. Plant garlic near tomatoes as a repellent. A jet of water during hot, dry weather may keep them off leaves, although roses in particular would not enjoy the bath.
	6. *Chemical control*: dicofol, malathion, more than one application may be necessary.

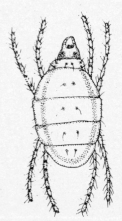

Spider Mites

Squash Vine Borer	1. The larvae aren't visible but the damage they do is apparent very quickly, when a whole squash vine wilts from one day to the next. 2. Can be found in many plants, but squash family vines are favoured. 3. *Organic control*: look along the vine or stem for the entry hole, often green castings are visible, then carefully slit the vine from the hole outward until you find the larva, then dig it (or them) out, and bury any part of the vine you opened, use Deritox Garden Guard. 4. *Chemical control*: Sevin, methoxy-chlor, Guard 'n Pride.

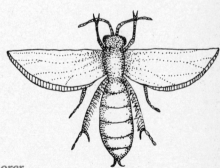

Squash Vine Borer

Tent Caterpillar

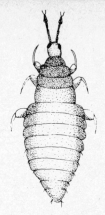

Thrips

Tent Caterpillar	1. These insects, like many others, seem to arrive in cycles, and in a bad year, they can defoliate a tree.
	2. Their spun tents are easy to see.
	3. All trees can be afflicted, even defoliated, particularly shade and fruit trees.
	4. *Organic control*: if the tent is within reach, take it down by hand at night and destroy it immediately, use Deritox Garden Guard.
	5. *Chemical control*: diazinon, Sevin.

Thrips	1. Very small, very active insects with piercing, sucking mouth parts.
	2. Suck plant juices especially in hot, dry weather.
	3. Attack all plants, especially gladioli where it leaves white strips on the leaves.
	4. *Organic control*: diatomaceous earth.
	5. *Chemical control*: Sevin, diazinon, Gardal Rose and Evergreen Dust.

Tomato Hornworm	1. A very large caterpillar (3 to 4 inches) that pretends it's a tomato vine stem while devouring the leaves, stems, and fruit of the tomato. 2. *Organic control*: BT (bacillus thuringiensis), remove by hand. 3. *Chemical control*: Sevin, diazinon, Tomato and Potato Dust (PTV Dust).

Weevil	1. Eats the leaf edges of bean and pea plants and lays its eggs in bean and pea flowers. 2. *Organic Control*: time the plantings so that the beans and peas flower before the adult insects lay eggs; find out from the Department of Agriculture when weevils are due to propagate in your area. 3. *Chemical Control*: carbaryl, malathion dust.

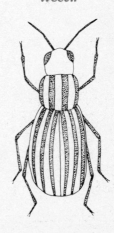

Weevil

Tomato Hornworm

Whiteflies	1. White insects gather beneath leaves and one good shake will produce a whole cloud of them from the leaves of tomatoes, fuchsias, mums, cucumbers and many other tender juicy plants. 2. Leaves will go off-colour. 3. Nasturtiums can attract whiteflies but stand up to considerable punishment from them. 4. Marigolds act as repellents. 5. *Organic control*: Deritox Garden Guard, pyrethrum. It has been discovered recently that a yellow ribbon suspended several feet above your crop will distract the whiteflies — coat the ribbon with honey or maple syrup and it will act like flypaper. 6. *Chemical control*: only the adult is vulnerable to pesticides, so spray is necessary at weekly intervals for about four weeks, use malathion, Banisect.

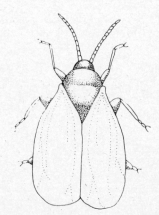

Whiteflies

Wireworms	1. Eat the roots of potatoes and carrots, lettuce, tomatoes and mums.
	2. Unfortunately, by the time the damage from this pest is noticed, you can't do much about it until the following season, although if you discover damage to lettuce or mums, you might be able to save nearby root vegetables.
	3. Regular cultivation keeps these under control, and are seldom a problem in well-established gardens.
	4. *Organic control*: bury potatoes around the garden, marking the spots with stakes, and then dig them up every two or three weeks, discarding and replacing any that have attracted wireworms.
	5. *Chemical control*: lindane (borer spray) or Banisect.

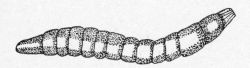

Wire Worms

Chapter Five

Diseases

Diseases

The function disease has in Nature's balance is to break down dead or unhealthy tissue into nutrients which can be taken up by new growth. Unfortunately, disease can spread to perfectly healthy plants with quite devastating consequences, such as the destruction of elm trees by the Dutch Elm disease.

The prevention of plant diseases is straightforward and, for the most part, highly effective. Keep your plants healthy and vigorous, without any stress from the wrong amount of nutrients, water and light. Cleanliness is next to healthiness. Remove all weak or broken plant parts and consistently pick up fallen leaves and other debris. Weed diligently. Weeds can carry disease and weaken the plants through competition. Insects can also carry disease so get rid of them as soon as possible.

New strains of plants are constantly being developed. Always buy disease-resistant varieties which have been certified, planting annuals in different places every year. Some sensitive plants and perennials, such as roses, will probably need regular applications of fungicide spray. It's a good idea to alternate suitable sprays so the disease won't have a chance to develop resistance.

When disease strikes, surgery is the most effective cure. As soon as you have identified a problem, remove any diseased plants or parts, burn them or throw them out immediately. Never put them on the compost heap. You should also disinfect the clippers or knife with a chlorine bleach and water solution before using again on healthy plants. Spray or dust the area with fungicide and re-examine your methods of cultivation. Chances are the diseased plant is suffering from some kind of stress and is not growing at full strength.

Here are some of the most common diseases you'll find in house-plants and backyard gardens. Some more complicated diseases might need expert help and very detailed examinations to identify. If you're having problems you can't solve, the experts at the nurseries, Department of Agriculture, or agricultural chemical companies will be glad to advise you.

Disease	Symptom and Control
Anthracnose	1. Brown-black spots on leaves of many different plants; privet and ficus very susceptible. 2. On beans, the pods are also affected. 3. On weeping willows, the stems on new growth can show symptoms as well. 4. Most prevalent in growing seasons which are cool and wet. 5. Remove and discard any infected parts but do not touch the leaves or harvest the beans if the plants are wet. 6. *Organic control*: rotate bean crops, use certified seed. Apply heavy dose of super phosphate; 1 pound per 100 square feet. 7. *Chemical control*: spray trees with Bordeaux mixture, Captan, Benomyl, or Zineb.
Black Spot	1. Black spots on leaves, often surrounded by yellow. 2. Frequently affects roses. 3. *Organic control*: remove all debris before protecting from winter weather: spray with organic dormant spray Lime Sulphur/Mineral Oil in early spring: boil rhubarb leaves in water and spray solution on rose leaves to prevent black spot. 4. *Chemical control*: starting when leaves open in spring, spray according to manufacturer's directions with Funginex, Benomyl, Captan, Gardal Rose and Flower Guard.

Disease	Symptom and Control
Blight	1. Begins as purple blotches on leaves of potatoes and tomatoes, which then turn brown and rot causing vegetables to rot as well. 2. Spray potatoes early, before they flower; tomatoes after the first fruit sets, and continue spraying once every two weeks during cool, wet summers. 3. *Organic control*: crop rotation, use certified disease-free stock, and control leafhoppers (with diazinon or Sevin) which carry the disease. 4. *Chemical control*: use Bordeaux mixture, maneb or zineb, or PTV Dust.
Blossom End Rot	1. Brown concave section on bottom of tomato. 2. Usually happens when a prolonged dry spell, which prevents the plant from getting sufficient calcium, is followed by heavy rain or excessive watering. 3. *Organic control*: prevent by regular watering so the roots never dry out, and by liming the soil to add calcium, or adding a liquid calcium supplement like Green Cross Tomato Food. 4. *Chemical control*: none.
Botrytis	1. Also called grey mold, it affects many plants in many different ways. 2. On fruit (beans, strawberries, tomatoes) it appears as a softening of the fruit under a powdery grey build-up.

Disease	Symptom and Control
Botrytis (Continued)	3. On flowers and leaves, it's a brown spotting followed by the powdery build-up and rotting (lettuce, chrysanthemums, hydrangeas, peonies). 4. On stems, the grey mold covers brown rotting areas (gooseberries, magnolias, roses). 5. Can also affect tubers and root crops in storage (tulips, onions). 6. *Organic control*: remove and discard any affected plants or parts, check humidity and ventilation. 7. *Chemical control*: spray with Benomyl, Captan, zineb, and treat bulbs with Bulb Dust fungicide before storage.
Clubroot	1. Wilting and yellowing of leaves caused by poor root action — roots become swollen and slimy. 2. Affects all members of the cabbage family (cabbage, broccoli, brussels sprouts, cauliflower) The disease remains in the soil for many years, so keep crop-free for a prolonged period of time. 3. *Organic control*: prevent by crop rotation, make sure soil pH does not drop below 7.0: discard afflicted plants: boil rhubarb leaves in water and pour solution into drills before planting susceptible plants: spread wood ash around base of susceptible plants at planting time.

Disease	Symptom and Control
Crown Gall	1. A cluster of yellow-brown lumps called galls that can grow to canteloupe size on the roots, and sometimes on the stems of roses, raspberries and blackberries. 2. If possible, remove galls — destroy severely afflicted plants. 3. Antibiotics (Bacticin, streptomycin) should be painted directly on the galls as soon as possible.
Damping-Off Disease	1. Newly sprouted seedlings or rooted cuttings weaken at the soil level, eventually falling over and breaking off. 2. Prevent by using sterilized soil mixture for propagation, water and mist seedlings early in the day so the soil surface dries before evening, and leave an inch or more between seedlings for air circulation. 3. *Organic control*: improve air circulation around susceptible plants, using a room fan if necessary: provide adequate sunshine or artificial light: reduce waterings and remove afflicted seedlings. 4. *Chemical control*: preventive fungicides like No-Damp are available and in early stages, damping-off can be arrested by adding Captan or zineb when watering seedlings.
Mildew (downy)	1. Downy mildew shows up as yellow spots on the surface of several vegetable leaves, with a white powdery build-up under the leaf. 2. Particularly susceptible are lettuce, cabbages, cucumbers, and grapes.

Disease	Symptom and Control
Mildew (Continued)	3. *Organic control*: prevent by rotating crops. 4. *Chemical control*: use maneb, zineb, or ziram on vegetables; Bordeaux mixture on grapes.
Mildew (powdery)	1. Powdery mildew is a fine white dust on the leaves and new growth of roses, begonias, lilacs, and grass; also on the fruit and leaves of apples and strawberries when the weather is wet and cool, particularly early and late in the season. 2. *Organic control*: remove afflicted areas if possible, reduce watering, and if problem exists in soil, add pulverized charcoal. 3. *Chemical control*: use sulphur on fruit, according to package directions. Spray ornamentals with Benomyl, dinocap or Funginex.
Rot	1. A general term applied to a group of diseases which usually affect the plants at the soil level, particularly bulbs, corms and tubers, and the crowns of some perennials — the leaves weaken, then topple over. 2. *Organic control*: good drainage, control of ground level pests such as slugs, and crop rotation when possible, can prevent rot: disease can also affect bulbs, corms, and tubers during storage so make sure they are dry before storing, and place in dry storage medium such as peat moss: check for rot during storage, remove afflicted bulbs, corms and tubers, and dust remainder with sulphur.

Disease	Symptom and Control
Rot (Continued)	3. *Chemical control*: remove afflicted plants, replace soil if problem is widespread: sterilize soil with oven heat for indoor plants, dust bulbs, corms and tubers with Captan, quintozene before planting.
Rust	1. Powdery rust-coloured spots on leaves of grass, particularly bluegrass, late in the growing season when weather turns cool and wet. 2. Some strains are resistant to rust, but when nitrogen is plentiful during growing season, all grasses are quite able to resist this disease. 3. *Organic control*: provide generous quantities of nitrogen. 4. *Chemical control*: apply maneb, or zineb when symptoms are first noticed and after heavy rains.
Snow Mold	1. Large dead patches in lawn, covered with white web-like mould, early in the spring. 2. All grasses can be affected. 3. *Organic control*: reduce application of fast-release nitrogen in late summer in growing season, and mow the lawn down short just before winter. 4. *Chemical control*: Benomyl, or thiram can be applied to turf, but grass usually recovers with nitrogen.
Verticillium Wilt	1. This, like fusarium wilt, causes many plants to wilt from the ground up. 2. Tomatoes are vulnerable but beans and peas can also be afflicted.

Disease	Symptom and Control
Verticillium (Continued)	3. There is no cure so plant resistant varieties and rotate crops to different parts of the garden every year. 4. When purchasing your seeds look for the letters VF indicating resistance to these two types of wilt.
Virus Diseases	1. Affect many plants in ways which resemble more common problems, like the yellowing of leaves, small irregularly-shaped leaves, small plants with weak flowers, small fruit, spindly stems or wilting. 2. Remove diseased parts and destroy immediately. 3. Be sure there is no other cause before removing. 4. Always plant certified disease-free stock, and kill insects which carry diseases, particularly aphids and leafhoppers, with regular applications of Sevin, or malathion.

Chapter Six

Using Chemicals

Using Chemicals

Every summer we hear stories about people who have misused agricultural chemicals in the garden. One gardener I know was spraying a broadleaf herbicide on his lawn, and decided that anything which was good for his lawn would be good for his trees as well, so he proceeded to spray the birches he had planted the year before. Of course they all perished. Gardeners have even put a weed-and-feed formula on their vegetable gardens in an attempt to fertilize their vegetables while controlling the weeds. Naturally, it destroyed all the vegetables along with the weeds, because it contained broadleaf herbicides which couldn't discriminate between a good vegetable and a bad weed.

Not all misuses are as obvious as these. I have heard stories of people who have sprayed the appropriate fungicide on their roses and wondered why they drooped and died. It was only after considerable investigation that they realized the sprayer they had used for the fungicide had contained weed killer some time before, and the residue was enough to kill the roses.

Before you use any chemicals in your garden you have to know what the chemical does, how it should be applied, how often, and in what concentration. You can obtain all the information you need from the labels. The companies which produce these chemical helpers can spend up to ten years and literally millions of dollars to find out this information so the least you can do is read it . . . for your own protection as well. Misuse of some chemicals can be hazardous to your health.

Make sure to read directions carefully before using chemicals.

Here are some guidelines:

1) Read the label, and follow the instructions accurately. Measure the chemical and the water you dissolve it in, and the area you are spraying.

2) Use separate sprayers for herbicides, and if you use a spray applicator for water soluble fertilizer, do not use that sprayer for any other chemical.

3) Rinse out sprayers after use. Some agricultural chemicals can dissolve rubber washers if left in contact.

4) Spray only those plants you want the chemical applied to. This is particularly important when using herbicides for the lawn near vegetables, flowers, or shrubs.

5) Watch the weather. Some chemicals are not effective if it rains too soon after they are applied. Wind can also cause sprays to drift into areas where they are not wanted which can be dangerous. Excessive heat and dryness can cause plants to overreact.

6) When control of pests or diseases involves regular spraying over the growing season, alternate types of sprays. Using the same ingredient all the time, particularly on mites, can cause a resistant strain to develop so the chemical will no longer have any effect.

7) On fruit and vegetable crops, follow instructions and make sure you leave enough time between the last application of chemical and the harvest to prevent chemical residue on your crops.

8) When spraying, avoid contact or inhalation of chemicals, and make sure children and animals are kept well away from the area.

9) After spraying, be sure to wash yourself well.

10) Store all agricultural chemicals in a dry place, locked away.

DANCING BEES

When a bee finds nectar, it needs to communicate all the necessary information to its fellow bees so it flies back to the hive and dances the details. The pattern and speed of the dance indicates whether the flowers are near or far, facing toward the sun or away from the sun, and other details to tell the bees exactly where to go.

Chemical Glossary

TRADE NAME	CHEMICAL	DESCRIPTION	DISTRIBUTOR
Banisect®	chlorpyrifos	broad spectrum insecticide especially good on soil insects: can also be used on household pests	Green Cross, CIBA-GEIGY Can. Ltd.
Benlate®	benomyl	systemic fungicide good for rose black spot, tomato leaf mold, mold and mildew on ornamental and fruit trees	Dupont Can. Ltd.
Bordeaux mixture	bordeaux mixture, a combination of copper sulphate and hydrated lime	a fungicide which should always be used alone: good on grape vines and mildew as it hardens up the leaves	Many distributors
Captan	captan	a fungicide which is hard on the eyes, nose and mouth but good for botrytis, rose black leaf, apple and pear scab, and soil-borne diseases	Many distributors
Cygon®2E	dimethoate	systemic insecticide especially good to eliminate birch leaf miners who get it through the leaves if you paint it on the trunk	Cyanamid Can. Inc.
Dacthal®	DCPA	pre-emergent crabgrass killer: area shouldn't be re-seeded for two months after	Green Cross, CIBA-GEIGY Can. Ltd.
Deritox Garden Guard®	rotenone (cubé root)	organic insecticide particularly good for insects on plants	Green Cross, CIBA-GEIGY Can. Ltd.
Diazinon	diazinon: in many forms and as an ingredient in other mixtures	full spectrum insecticide	Many distributors
Funginex®	triforine	fungicide good for black spot, mold and mildew	Celamerck, G. mbH and Co. KG

TRADE NAME	CHEMICAL	DESCRIPTION	DISTRIBUTOR
Gardal Rose & Evergreen dust™	captan, malathion, carbaryl, thiophanate-methyl	systemic fungicide for bugs and diseases on roses, ornamentals, and evergreens	Green Cross, CIBA-GEIGY Can. Ltd.
Guard 'n' Pride™	malathion, dichlone, methoxychlor	insecticide/fungicide which kills insects and controls diseases at the same time	Green Cross, CIBA-GEIGY Can. Ltd.
Killex®	2,4-D, mecoprop, dicamba	herbicide for all broadleafed weeds, unwanted grasses: apply carefully when it is not hot or windy and keep off wanted plants	Green Cross, CIBA-GEIGY Can. Ltd.
Maneb	maneb	fungicide to control rose black spot, potato blight, and tomato leaf mold and blight	Many distributors
PTV Dust®	carbaryl, zeneb	fungicide for both insects and diseases: particularly good for potatoes	King Bug Killer
Sevin®	carbaryl	broad spectrum insecticide, especially effective on beetles: safe near pets and children, but don't use near honey-bees	Union Carbide Can. Ltd.
Trump™	mesurol	slug and snail bait	Green Cross, CIBA-GEIGY Can. Ltd.
Weed Guard™	chloramben	herbicide useful for killing weeds in flower and vegetable gardens	Green Cross, CIBA-GEIGY Can. Ltd.
Weed-No-More®	2,4-D	herbicide effective on dandelions and plaintains: keep away from wanted grass	Green Cross, CIBA-GEIGY Can. Ltd.
Zineb	zineb	fungicide for diseases of ornamental and fruit trees: also good for vegetables	Many distributors

Notes

Notes

Cullen Garden Guides

HOUSEPLANTS by Mark Cullen

A concise guide to maintaining your houseplants. Includes information on care (water, fertilizer, light), propagation (seeds, offsets, transplanting, repotting), and techniques such as hydroponics and interior landscaping. Includes a troubleshooting chart on plant problems and solutions. **$5.95**

LAWNS AND LANDSCAPING by Mark Cullen

A concise guide on planting, refurbishing and maintaining lawns. Includes information on starting new lawns, maintainence (mowing, watering, fertilizing), and weed and disease control. Additionally there is a complete section on the use of trees and bushes to landscape your yard. **$5.95**

VEGETABLES AND BUSH FRUITS by Mark Cullen

A concise guide on home growing of vegetables and fruits. Includes information on choice of types for Canadian climate, techniques (seed, transplanting), maintaining (watering, fertilizer, mid-season care). **$5.95**

WEEDS, PESTS AND DISEASES by Mark Cullen

A concise guide on the control of all undesirables in lawns, flowers, trees and all plants in your home. Includes descriptions of weeds and pests, and explains their habits and methods of control. Recommends use of organic methods, or various herbicides and pesticides. **$5.95**

If you can't find your favourite Cullen Garden Guide where you shop, you can obtain a copy by sending **$5.95** plus **50¢** postage for each book to:

Summerhill Press Ltd.
5 Clarence Square
Toronto, Ontario M5V 1H1

Please allow three weeks for delivery